The Power of
The Counties

The Power of
The Counties
Laurence Waters

An imprint of
Ian Allan Publishing

Half-title:
Despite being the test locomotive, No 1009 was actually the second 'County' to be fitted with the new-pattern elliptical double chimney in September 1956. (The first was No 1022, in May 1956.) It is seen in its new guise leaving Parson's Tunnel, near Teignmouth, with the 7.30am service from Paddington to Plymouth on 16 April 1957. *W. N. Lockett*

Frontispiece:
An early view of No 1029 *County of Worcester*, emerging from the tunnel under the city wall at Chester with a service from Birkenhead to Paddington. It has been fitted with a smokebox numberplate but as yet does not have a shedplate. *Eric Treacy*

Title page:
A works-posed photograph of No 1019 *County of Merioneth* taken at Swindon in February 1949. The locomotive is in full BR mixed-traffic lined black, being the first 'County' to be painted in this livery following Nationalisation, but has black backgrounds to its name- and numberplates. Note the NA (Newton Abbot) shed code stencilled on the front buffer-beam in Great Western style. *Ian Allan Library*

First published 2006

ISBN (10) 0 86093 604 X
ISBN (13) 978 0 86093 604 6

© Ian Allan Publishing Ltd 2006

Published by Oxford Publishing Co

an imprint of Ian Allan Publishing Ltd, Hersham, Surrey KT12 4RG.
Printed in England by Ian Allan Printing Ltd, Hersham, Surrey KT12 4RG.

Code: 0610/B

Visit the Ian Allan Publishing website at www.ianallanpublishing.com

Introduction

There is no doubt that one of the most important features of the Great Western Railway, from its formation in 1835 right through until nationalisation in 1948, was the continuous development and subsequent standardisation of locomotive design. This was due in no small measure to the fact that, over the whole of the company's 112-year existence, locomotive policy was effectively in the hands of just six chief mechanical engineers.

Daniel Gooch was the first Locomotive Superintendent to be appointed by the GWR, holding the position from 1837 to 1864. The next in line was Joseph Armstrong, who occupied the post of 'Locomotive and Carriage Superintendent' from 1864 to 1877. William Dean was appointed to this title in 1877 and was superseded in 1902 by George Jackson Churchward, who served until 1921. Charles Benjamin Collett held the post from 1922 until 1941, the last CME being Frederick William Hawksworth, 1941 to 1949. The title 'Locomotive Superintendent' had been changed to 'Chief Mechanical Engineer' in 1916, but essentially the job remained the same. Hawksworth retired from British Railways (Western Region) at the end of 1949, after which the position of CME was abolished.

F. W. Hawksworth, who was to be responsible for the introduction of the 'County'-class 4-6-0s, was born in Swindon on 10 February 1884. His father was employed by the GWR's Swindon drawing office, while his grandfather was the workshop foreman at Shrewsbury locomotive depot. The young Hawksworth attended Sanford Street School in Swindon and had his introduction to steam while on holiday in Wales, with trips on his grandfather's steam launch. Thus it was no great surprise when Hawksworth junior continued the family tradition by joining the Great Western as an apprentice at Swindon Locomotive Works, on 1 August 1898. Over the ensuing years he served in a variety of jobs, one of which was in the engine-testing house, a good grounding for a future Chief Mechanical Engineer. During his apprenticeship he attended the Swindon Technical Institute and was awarded the Gooch Prize for machine drawing. He also received the Chairman's Prize for the highest aggregation marks.

In 1905 Hawksworth was appointed to the position of Draughtsman and joined his father in the drawing office. He continued his education, obtaining a 1st-class honours degree in machine design at the Royal College of Science. Promotion on the Great Western was slow, and it was not until 1923 that he attained the position of Assistant Chief Draughtsman to O. E. F. Deverell; two years later, on Deverell's retirement, he was promoted to Chief Draughtsman.

In 1932 William (later Sir William) Stanier, at this time principal assistant to C. B. Collett, left the GWR to join the London, Midland & Scottish Railway as Chief Mechanical Engineer, and later the same year Hawksworth took over as Collett's principal assistant. With his long service at Swindon he was well qualified for the job, and

when Collett retired in 1941 at the age of 70, Hawksworth, who was by now 57 years of age, was appointed, on 5 July, to the post of Chief Mechanical Engineer.

Nationalisation of the railways at the beginning of 1948 gave Hawksworth the distinction of being the last CME of the Great Western Railway, and he retired two years later, on 31 December 1949. Just like Collett before him he was a great admirer of Churchward and his locomotive designs, and during his career at Swindon he had risen from the bottom of the ladder right to the very top. It could be said that Nationalisation came too soon for Hawksworth, and this, together with his subsequent retirement, meant that in many areas of locomotive design he really did not fulfil his ambitions. He died on 13 July

1976 at the ripe old age of 92, but his memory lives on in Swindon, for, as a permanent mark of respect, Swindon Borough Council perpetuated his name in a development on ex-railway land.

The development of the 'County' class

Hawksworth took on the role of Chief Mechanical Engineer at a difficult time for the Great Western. Not only was Britain in the throws of war with Germany, but GWR locomotive policy was being controlled by the Mechanical Engineers' Committee of the wartime Railway Executive. This resulted in orders for 4-6-0s such as 'Castles', 'Manors' being cancelled. Instead, work at Swindon was concentrated on the construction of mixed-traffic and freight locomotives, including 80 Stanier-designed LMS '8F' 2-8-0s, built in 1943/4. Construction of Great Western locomotives did not cease completely, however, a number of '2251', '2884', '42xx' and '57xx' types being built, as were 72 Collett-designed '49xx' 'Hall' 4-6-0s, produced in small batches between November 1939 and April 1943.

One of the many problems for the railways at this time was the variable quality of the coal being supplied, much of

it being of a poor standard. This resulted in bad steaming, with the consequent poor performance and timekeeping, and caused many problems for locomotive crews and operating staff. On the Great Western, Hawksworth and his team were actively looking at ways of improving locomotive performance, while having to use poor quality coal. One solution was to move away from the railway's standard practice by developing a higher degree of superheat. Another consideration at this time was an acute shortage of shed staff and other labour, so any new locomotive design had to incorporate features that would provide for easier servicing and accessibility of working parts.

The war meant that any new locomotive designing was severely curtailed, but in 1944, with the war going well, a decision was made to construct a further batch of 'Hall' 4-6-0s. This allowed Hawksworth to incorporate a number of his own ideas in their construction, including the introduction of improved superheating. This was obtained by fitting a new-design three-row superheater with a header regulator within the Swindon standard No 1 boiler.

The first of the 'Modified Halls', No 6959 *Peatling Hall*, was completed in March 1944, a further 70 examples beingconstructed at Swindon between March 1944 and November 1950. Apart from the three-row superheater, the class was also fitted with a number of other Hawksworth design features, including plate frames, new-pattern cylinders and a plate-frame bogie. Later engines were also turned out with Hawksworth-designed straight-sided

tenders. In use the 'Modified Halls' were very successful and showed a marked improvement in performance over the Collett-designed originals.

In 1945 Hawksworth took the two-cylinder passenger 4-6-0 design a step further with the construction of the 'County' class. Just as the 'King' was the final development of the 'Star' 4-6-0, the Hawksworth 'County' can be regarded as the final development of the 'Saint', the classic two-cylinder Great Western 4-6-0 design introduced by G.-J. Churchward in 1902. To all intents and purposes the 'County' was a modern enlarged 'Saint' but still within the 20-ton axle load limit.

The 'Counties' carried over a number of features that Hawksworth had used on his 'Modified Halls', including frames made from plate steel and cylinders that were cast separately. The front bogie was also constructed of steel plate. The front of the boiler and smokebox were mounted

on a fabricated-steel saddle support. Fuel, comprising 7 tons of coal and 4,000 gallons of water, was carried in a new-design flat-sided tender of much simpler construction, the tank being welded rather than riveted. One major difference from other Great Western 4-6-0s was the provision of an 8ft 6in-wide cab.

The new class was fitted with 6ft 3in driving wheels and a Swindon-designed No 15 boiler, which was built to operate at 280lb pressure, the highest on the Great Western Railway. The new boiler was very similar to that used on the LMS Stanier-designed '8F' 2-8-0s, as per the batch built at Swindon during the war. The firebox and boiler barrel dimensions were the same, but the 'County' boiler was 9in longer. In order to save on costs Swindon had made use of the existing '8F' flanging blocks in the production of the firebox throat and back plates. Modified staying was also incorporated, to allow for the higher boiler pressure. Ease of servicing was an important consideration, and this was helped by the provision of a new hopper-type ash pan, which allowed the quicker removal of ash during depot visits.

The first member of the class, No 1000 *County of Middlesex*, was turned out from Swindon on 4 August 1945. It was fitted from new with a double blastpipe and a copper-capped double chimney for experimental purposes, all other members of the class being built with single chimneys.

With a high nominal tractive effort of 32,580lb at 85% boiler pressure the 'Counties' were the most powerful

Above:
The Swindon No 15 boiler fitted to the 'Counties' was based on that of the Stanier-designed '8F' 2-8-0. They shared the same firebox and boiler barrel dimensions, but the 'County' boiler was 9in longer. Here, ex-LMS '8F' No 48727 approaches Oxford on 27 July 1963 with a Washwood Heath–Hinksey Yard freight. It is coupled to a narrow, Fowler-design tender. *D. Tuck / Great Western Trust collection*

two-cylinder 4-6-0s on the Great Western. They were similar in power to the four-cylinder 'Castle' class 4-6-0s, but by virtue of their two-cylinder layout the 'Counties' were cheaper both to build and to maintain. The principal dimensions of No 1000, as built, were as follows:

Cylinders	18½in diameter x 30in stroke
Coupled wheels	6ft 3in diameter
Heating surfaces	
Tubes	1,545sq ft
Superheaters	265sq ft
Firebox	169sq ft
Total	1,979sq ft
Firegrate area	28.84sq ft
GWR power and route classification	E Red (later D Red)
BR power classification	6MT

Above:
The first 'County' 4-6-0, No 1000, was completed at Swindon on 4 August 1945. This official works picture shows the locomotive shortly after completion and as yet unnamed. The unique experimental copper-capped double chimney can be seen to good effect. *Great Western Trust collection*

Below:
Another official works picture of No 1000 *County of Middlesex,* taken shortly after it was named in March 1946. The locomotive is in prewar fully lined green livery, with the later design of Great Western crest on the tender. *Great Western Trust collection*

An unusual feature for a Great Western 4-6-0 was the use of continuous wheel splashers and straight nameplates. On the left-hand side of the locomotive the nameplate was fitted directly to the splasher; on the right side the plate was fitted on an extended backplate to clear the reversing lever, which ran outside the splasher. The continuous splasher and straight nameplates were similar in style to those fitted during 1935 on partially streamlined 'King' No 6014 *King Henry VII* and 'Castle' No 5005 *Manorbier*

Castle; Hawksworth was Collett's assistant at this time, and with his previous experience he probably had some input into their design, and it is interesting to speculate whether this had an influence in his use of a similar style of splasher and nameplate on the 'County' class.

History has recorded that the 'Counties' were not as successful as they might have been. One problem was that an increase in power on a two-cylinder design sometimes resulted in a rough ride. The class also inflicted heavy

Above:
No 1000 waits at Paddington with the 4.20pm service to Cheltenham, for its return to Swindon. It had worked up to London on the 10.53am service from Swindon, which was its inaugural run, on 13 August 1945. *Great Western Trust collection*

Right:
Another view of No 1000 on the same day, prior to the run back to Swindon. On the footplate, from left to right, are F. W. Hawksworth, Sir James Milne, Lord Portal, and Driver C. W. Brown, of Swindon. It is not recorded whether any of the VIPs rode on the footplate during the journey to Swindon. *Great Western Trust collection*

hammer-blow on the track, which, of course, did not go down well with the Civil Engineer. That notable railway writer, the late O. S. Nock, considered that on fast express services they were not as free-running as a 'Castle'. However, with their smaller driving wheels and extra power they always had a good acceleration and hill-climbing ability, making them popular with locomotive crews. With an axle weight of 19 tons 14cwt, the 'Counties' were initially restricted to the main lines between Paddington and Penzance and Paddington and Wolverhampton but were subsequently allowed to run over most other Great Western main lines, subject to speed restrictions.

Over the years, in both single- and double-chimney form, the class proved to be good, reliable performers on services in West Wales, the South West of England and on the route between Wolverhampton and Chester. They also performed well on cross-country services, particularly the

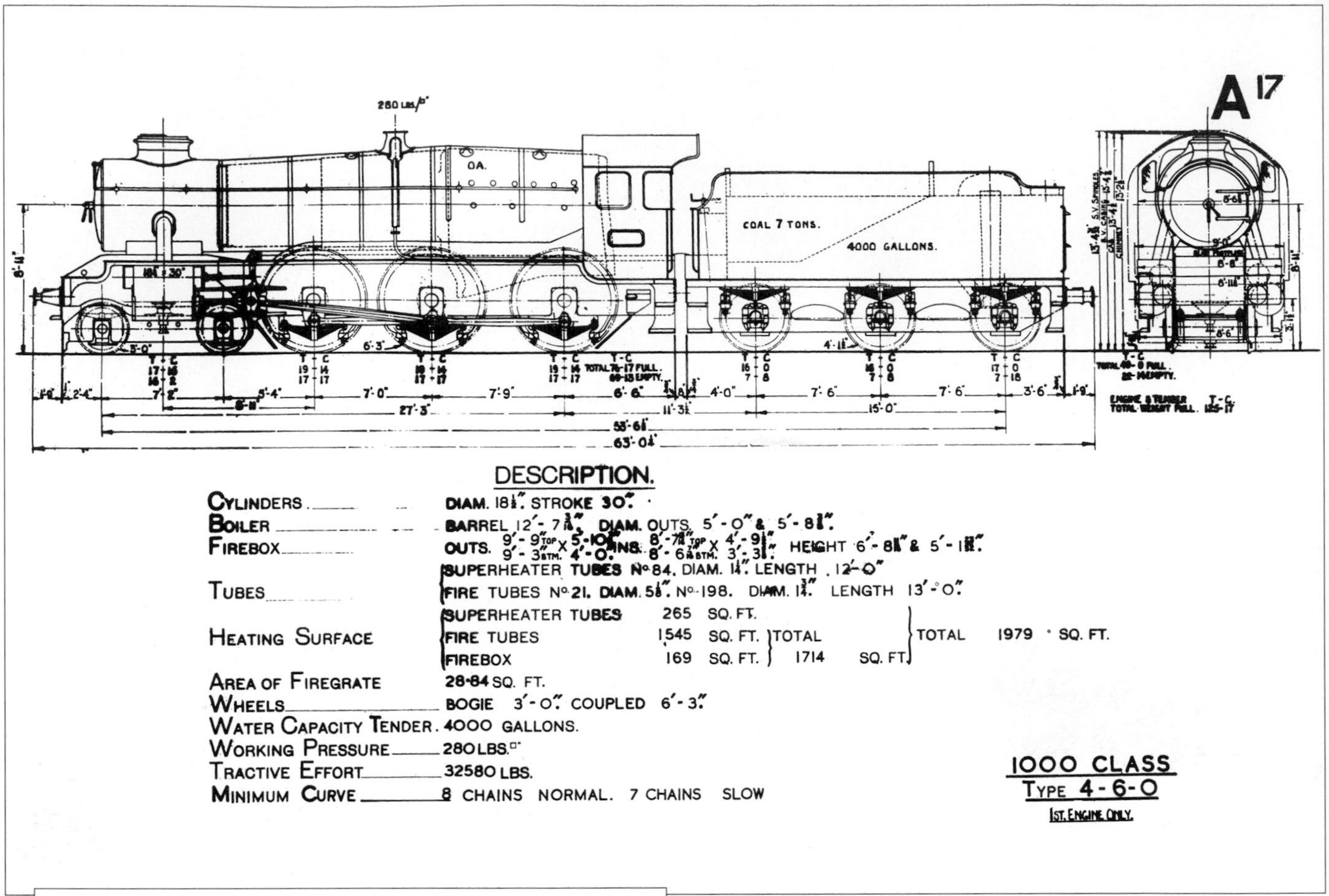
A17
280 LBS/□"
COAL 7 TONS.
4000 GALLONS.
DESCRIPTION.
CYLINDERS DIAM. 18½" STROKE 30"
BOILER BARREL 12'-7⅜" DIAM. OUTS. 5'-0" & 5'-8⅜"
FIREBOX OUTS. 9'-9" TOP 9'-3" BTM. X 5'-10" 4'-0" INS. 8'-7⅞" TOP 8'-6⅛" BTM. X 4'-9⅛" 3'-3⅛" HEIGHT 6'-8⅛" & 5'-1⅞"
TUBES SUPERHEATER TUBES No 84. DIAM. 1¼" LENGTH 12'-0"
FIRE TUBES No 21. DIAM. 5⅛". No 198. DIAM. 1⅞" LENGTH 13'-0"
HEATING SURFACE SUPERHEATER TUBES 265 SQ. FT.
FIRE TUBES 1545 SQ. FT. TOTAL 1714 SQ. FT.
FIREBOX 169 SQ. FT.
TOTAL 1979 SQ. FT.
AREA OF FIREGRATE 28·84 SQ. FT.
WHEELS BOGIE 3'-0" COUPLED 6'-3"
WATER CAPACITY TENDER. 4000 GALLONS.
WORKING PRESSURE 280 LBS.□"
TRACTIVE EFFORT 32580 LBS.
MINIMUM CURVE 8 CHAINS NORMAL. 7 CHAINS SLOW
1000 CLASS
TYPE 4-6-0
1ST. ENGINE ONLY.

Diagram showing the dimensions of the 'County' 4-6-0s.

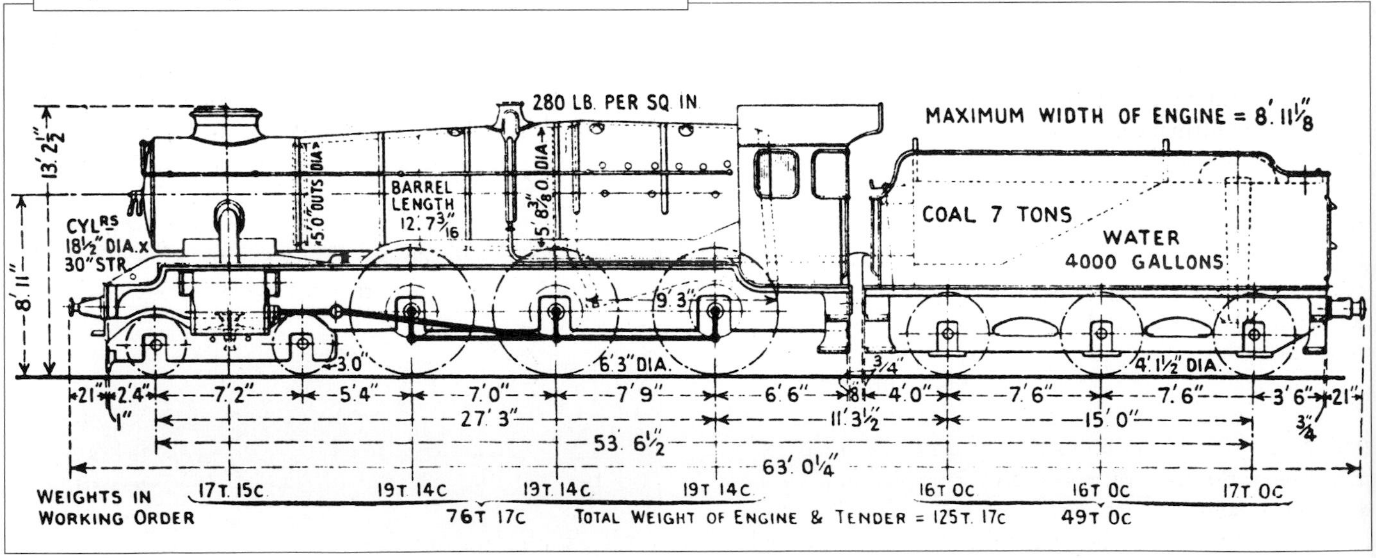
280 LB. PER SQ IN
MAXIMUM WIDTH OF ENGINE = 8'. 11⅛"
13'. 2½"
CYLRS 18½" DIA. X 30" STR
8'. 11"
5'.0" OUTS DIA
BARREL LENGTH 12'. 7³⁄₁₆"
5'. 8⅜" DIA
COAL 7 TONS
WATER 4000 GALLONS
3'.0"
6'.3" DIA.
9'.3"
4'. 1½" DIA.
WEIGHTS IN WORKING ORDER
17T. 15C
19T 14C
19T. 14C
19T 14C
16T 0C
16T 0C
17T 0C
76T 17C
TOTAL WEIGHT OF ENGINE & TENDER = 125T. 17C
49T 0C
27'. 3"
53'. 6½"
63'. 0¼"
11'. 3½"
15'. 0"

route from Chester to the South West via Hereford, Abergavenny and Bristol.

In 1954 a series of steam and rolling tests were carried out at Swindon by a team led by Sam Ell, who at this time was in charge of locomotive testing. Much of the work centred on the need to improve boiler performance when faced with the continuing problem of inferior coal supplies. The first tests were carried out using No 1000 *County of Middlesex*, which, even with the benefit of its early-pattern experimental double chimney, still suffered from poor steaming; apparently, this locomotive had always suffered from a problem in balancing the blast to the steaming requirements, and when it was being worked hard, as was often the case, the fireman had difficulty maintaining a good fire.

In September 1954 further draughting tests were carried out using No 1009 *County of Carmarthen*, which was fitted with an experimental fabricated sheet-steel stovepipe double chimney. After a period of extensive testing, a number of draughting improvements were made to the 'Counties', and between 1956 and 1959 all were fitted with a new-design elliptical double chimney (very similar in style to that used

Above:

In November 1954 No 1009 *County of Carmarthen* was fitted with an experimental stovepipe double chimney and underwent extensive testing in order to improve its steaming performance. It is seen here with its strange-looking chimney departing from Swindon on one such test run. The faces of the test staff looking out of the two front portholes of the wooden inspection shelter are just visible; it must have been hot in there! As a result of these tests the whole class were fitted with a new-design double chimney and four-row superheaters. *R. C. H. Nash / Great Western Trust collection*

on the 'King' class) and four-row superheaters. At the same time boiler pressure was reduced by 30lb to 250lb, which effectively reduced tractive effort to 29,090lb. The first member of the class to be fitted with the elliptical double chimney was No 1022 *County of Northampton*, in May 1956, the last being No 1021 *County of Montgomery* in October 1959. The modifications certainly improved steaming efficiency and the overall performance of the class, but to many Great Western purists the squat chimney ruined the look of these locomotives.

None of the class survived until the end of steam working on the Western Region. The first withdrawals took place in September 1962, when Nos 1004/18/26 were condemned, and by the end of the year they had been joined by Nos 1003/7/15/7/22/9. A further 13 locomotives, Nos 1001/2/5/6/8/9/16/9/21/3/5/7/8, were

withdrawn in 1963, leaving just eight members of the class to survive until 1964. These did not last much longer, and by July Nos 1000/10/2-4/20/4 had been placed in store. The last working example, No 1011 *County of Chester*, was spruced up in order to haul the 'County Farewell' railtour from Birmingham to Swindon on 20 September 1964. It continued working for several weeks after this, mainly in the Swindon and Bristol areas, before being withdrawn in November and put into store at Swindon. It finally ended up at Cashmore's, Newport, but was not cut up until March 1965.

Liveries

All members of the class were turned out from new in GWR lined-green livery. No 1000 *County of Middlesex* was, however, the only example to be fully lined, with cylinders, footplate valences and tender-frame valences outlined in chrome orange.

After Nationalisation in 1948 the 'Counties' were gradually painted in BR mixed-traffic lined black, with 'BRITISH RAILWAYS' painted on the tender. About half were turned out from Swindon with red-backed nameplates and cabside numberplates, but this practice was abandoned in June 1950, after which the backgrounds to the plates were painted black. For a short while in 1948 Nos 1009 and 1017 ran with a temporary 'W' suffix painted beneath their numberplates.

The next livery change occurred when, from May 1955, as they passed through works, the entire class was repainted in fully lined BR Brunswick green.

Above:
A works photograph taken in September 1950 showing
No 1019 *County of Merioneth* resplendent in British
Railways mixed-traffic lined black, a livery eventually
applied to the whole class. The backgrounds of the name-
and numberplates are painted red. The forward-facing
footstep on the right-hand buffer-beam was a feature of
the Hawksworth 'Counties'. *Ian Allan Library*

Names and numbers

The original intention was that the 'Counties' should be
numbered 9900-29 in the Great Western mixed-traffic 4-6-0
numbering scheme. It has been suggested that the decision
to number them in this series was leaked to an enthusiasts'
journal, whereupon the outcry was such that the Great
Western relented and numbered them 1000-29 — a nice
story if true. The August and September 1945 issues of the
Great Western Railway Magazine describe the new
locomotives as the '1000' class, with no mention of what the
naming policy might be. A full list of county names selected
to be used is contained in a letter, dated 7 January 1946,
from Hawksworth to K. J. Cook, the Works Manager, with
the added instruction to fit nameplates to those members of
the class already in service. In the event Nos 1000-18 were
all turned out from Swindon without names.

Interestingly, on the CME's list No 1007 is shown as
County of Brecon, but this has been crossed out and altered
to *County of Brecknock*. No 1011 is listed as *County of
Cheshire*, a name originally carried by Churchward
'County' 4-4-0 No 3814 until altered to *County of Chester*
in 1907. There was obviously still some dispute in 1946
over the use of 'Cheshire' or 'Chester', and a note from the

Town Clerk of Chester states that the correct title is
actually the 'County Palatine of Chester'; eventually
No 1011 was named simply *County of Chester*.

Naming was quite sporadic. The first member of the
class, No 1000, completed on 4 August 1945, was named
County of Middlesex at Paddington in March 1946.
No 1006 *County of Cornwall*, completed on 15 November
1945, ran the longest without nameplates, not being
named until 22 April 1948. No 1010, named *County of
Carnarvon* on 16 December 1947, had its plates altered
to *County of Caernarvon* on 14 November 1951.

Between Nationalisation and about May 1951
all members of the class were fitted with smokebox
numberplates and BR shedcode plates.

Tenders

The first batch of tenders was built at Swindon Works
under Lot No 180 and numbered 2935-54 but were later
renumbered 100-19; the second batch was built under Lot
No 183 and numbered 120-9. These tenders incorporated
a number of new design features over the standard Collett
4,000-gallon tender. The 'County' tenders held 4,000
gallons of water and 7 tons of coal and were flush-
bottomed, with straight sides that were higher than those
of the standard Collett type. They were built using welded
rather than riveted construction and had a total weight in
full working order of 49 tons.

The same design was used by Hawksworth on his
'Modified Halls' from No 6971 *Athelhampton Hall*.
The design was also used on the final batch of 'Castles',
but those for the 'Counties', at 8ft 6in wide, were 6in
wider than those fitted to the other locomotives.

The 1014 *County of Glamorgan* project

In December 2004 an agreement was reached between the Vale of Glamorgan Council, the Heritage Lottery Fund and the Great Western Society to construct a full-size working replica of Hawksworth 'County' 4-6-0 No 1014 *County of Glamorgan*. Much of the work will be undertaken at Didcot Railway Centre, using the frames of 'Modified Hall' No 7927 *Willington Hall* and the boiler from Stanier '8F' No 48518, which will be converted into a Swindon No 15 OB boiler. Many other items, including the 6ft 3in driving wheels and a flat-sided tender, will have to be fabricated from new.

The new 'County' will be built to run in its ultimate form, with the later-type double chimney and blastpipe and a four-row superheater. Work on the project has already started, and one hopes that in a few years' time it will once again be possible to see a Hawksworth 'County' in action.

Acknowledgements

I should like to thank the following for their help: Hugh Ballantyne, Robin Isaac, Phillip Kelley, Michael Mensing, the late Ivo Peters, Bill Peto, Norman Preedy, Tony Rivers, Peter Treloar, Peter Waller, the Great Western Trust and the Ian Allan Library.

As always, the RCTS *Locomotives of the Great Western Railway* series has proved an invaluable source of information.

Laurence Waters
August 2006

Note: Locomotive shed allocations, mileages and repair details used in this book are taken from the official GWR/Western Region records held at the National Archive, Kew, and from other documents held by the Great Western Trust at Didcot. Total mileages quoted are up to 28 December 1963 only, as figures were not recorded by the Western Region after that date.

Below:
A 'County' in its final form. No 1003 *County of Wilts*, stands outside the works at Swindon after a heavy general repair, on 7 November 1957. It has been fitted with the new squat-design elliptical double chimney and is painted in fully lined BR Brunswick green. *Great Western Trust collection*

1000 *County of Middlesex*

Built	Swindon, August 1945
Named	March 1946
Double chimney fitted	from new
Allocations	Old Oak Common from new
	Plymouth Laira, December 1951
	Chester, October 1952
	Bristol Bath Road, March 1954
	Bristol St Philip's Marsh,
	September 1960
Withdrawn	6 July 1964
Final mileage	733,933
Cut up	J. Cashmore, Newport, December 1964

Above:
In October 1952 *County of Middlesex* was allocated to Chester (84K) and is seen under the overall roof at Shrewsbury on the 29th, having arrived with an up service from Birkenhead to Paddington. This roof was removed during the 1960s. *R. O. Tuck*

Below:
County of Middlesex was fitted with the new, squat design of elliptical double chimney in March 1958, when it was in the works for a heavy general repair. It is seen here in Swindon Works yard at that time, newly repainted in fully lined BR Brunswick green. *Great Western Trust collection*

Above:
No 1000 and ex-Great Western 'Castle' class 4-6-0 No 4073 *Caerphilly Castle* stand alongside the coaling plant at Swansea Landore on 30 March 1958. Although it did not achieve the highest mileage, this locomotive was in service longer than any of the other member of the class. *P. J. Kelley*

Below:
From March 1960 until its withdrawal in July 1964 No 1000 was allocated to Bristol Bath Road (82A) and latterly to St Philip's Marsh (82B). It is seen here in a less than pristine condition, in November 1963, as it passes through Didcot with a down milk train. It was withdrawn from 82B on 6 July 1964. *I. J. Hodson*

1001 *County of Bucks*

Built	Swindon, September 1945
Named	December 1947
Double chimney fitted	December 1957
Allocations	Newton Abbot from new
	Neyland, August 1949
	Penzance, March 1960
	Didcot, February 1961
	Neyland, September 1962
Withdrawn	24 May 1963
Final mileage	664,361
Cut up	J. Cashmore, Newport, May 1964

Above:
No 1001 was completed at Swindon on 4 September 1945. From new it was allocated to Newton Abbot, and is seen here unnamed at Penzance shed during the summer of 1947. It was named *County of Bucks* on 9 December that year. *Great Western Trust collection*

Below:
Another early view of No 1001, again, still unnamed, at Plymouth. The lack of nameplate enables the single splasher and the outside reversing lever on the right-hand side to be seen clearly. *Great Western Trust collection*

Above:
During August 1949, *County of Bucks* moved from the South West of England to West Wales when reallocated to Neyland where it stayed until March 1960. Judging by the lack of photographs unearthed in researching this book the locomotive was an elusive one for photographers but is seen here at Carmarthen on 24 June 1955.
F. M. Gates / Great Western Trust collection

Left:
In 1955 No 1001 was sent for repair to Caerphilly Works, where it was photographed in the erecting shop on 30 December. This was the first occasion that a 'County' class 4-6-0 was repaired here and only three other members of the class underwent repair at this works: No 1029 in December 1957, No 1017 in July 1959, and No 1005 in August 1960.
E. Mountford / Great Western Trust collection

Above:
When repairs had been completed at Caerphilly, *County of Bucks* was steam tested in the works yard as seen here on 4 January 1956, newly repainted in BR lined-green. Its double chimney was fitted at Swindon Works in December 1957. *E. Mountford / Great Western Trust collection*

Below:
After spending a year back in the South West working from Penzance (83G) *County of Bucks* returned to Neyland, being reallocated to there on 7 September 1962 as depicted on the 21st of the same month, once again carrying an 87H shedplate. It is probably preparing to leave with the 2.20pm service to Paddington. This locomotive was withdrawn from service on 24 May 1963. *F. K. Davies / Great Western Trust collection*

Below:

As yet unnamed, Bristol Bath Road-allocated No 1002 stands at Taunton on 29 July 1946 with an up express service. Completed on 27 September 1945, it was named *County of Berks* on 21 May 1947. The reversing lever can be seen, and as already mentioned, this required the right-hand nameplate to be fitted on a raised bracket in front of the lever. Although seemingly dirty, the locomotive is in GW lined-green livery.
J. Alves / Great Western Trust collection

1002 *County of Berks*	
Built	Swindon, September 1945
Named	May 1947
Double chimney fitted	June 1958
Allocations	Bristol Bath Road from new
	Plymouth Laira, February 1953
	Penzance, November 1953
	St Blazey, June 1961
	Penzance, November 1961
	Didcot, May 1962
	Shrewsbury, October 1962
Withdrawn	17 September 1963
Final mileage	766,263
Cut up	T. W. Ward, Sheffield, January 1964

Below:

After Nationalisation the 'Counties' were painted in BR mixed-traffic lined-black livery. This can be seen to good effect on *County of Berks* as it stands at Bristol Temple Meads after arriving with a down service from London in 1949. As yet there is no crest on the tender, and the name and numberplates are picked out in red. Smokebox numberplates were fitted to the 'Counties' from about 1950, and all had received them by May 1951.
Ian Allan Library

Above:
In spotless condition, Penzance (83G)-allocated *County of Berks* leaves Buckshead Tunnel, Truro, on 18 September 1957 with the up 'Royal Duchy', the 11am restaurant-car service from Penzance to London. The class proved to be good performers in the South West. *P. Q. Treloar*

Right:
Another Penzance working was the up 'Cornishman', the 10.30am service from Penzance to Wolverhampton, as far as Plymouth. The train is depicted arriving at Par on 18 May 1959 hauled by *County of Berks*. The locomotive is in lined-green livery, as applied to the class from May 1955, and is fitted with a double chimney, which it received in June 1958. *Michael Mensing*

Left:
County of Berks was reallocated to Shrewsbury in October 1962, being observed subsequently undergoing running repairs at Oswestry shed. It was withdrawn from Shrewsbury in September 1963. *E. N. Kneale*

Below:
A clean-looking No 1002 waits at Penzance on 13 June 1958 with the 10.5am service to Manchester. The locomotive had only recently been fitted with a double chimney at Swindon but had obviously not had a complete repaint as the tender retains the early BR lion-and-wheel emblem. *J. Aston / Great Western Trust collection*

1003 *County of Wilts*

Built	Swindon, October 1945
Named	August 1947
Double chimney fitted	November 1957
Allocations	Old Oak Common from new
	Plymouth Laira, December 1950
	Shrewsbury, April 1951
Withdrawn	22 October 1962
Final mileage	655,000
Cut up	J. Cashmore, Newport, May 1964

Above:
Old Oak Common-allocated No 1003 *County of Wilts*
waits at Newport on 16 June 1950 with the 1.55pm service
from Paddington to West Wales. Completed at Swindon on
2 October 1945, it was not named until 9 August 1947.
P. Q. Treloar collection

Below:
County of Wilts speeds through the Thames Valley in the
early 1950s on a down fast service from Paddington.
Great Western Trust collection

Left:
This rare view shows *County of Wilts* in newly applied BR lined-black livery in the main erecting shop at Swindon in January 1951. It is carrying a Plymouth Laira (83D) shedplate, and although it was only at this depot from December 1950 until April 1951, it spent most of this time in the works at Swindon having a heavy general repair. It left the works on 16 April and was then reallocated to Shrewsbury (84G). *P. Q. Treloar*

Below:
The Shrewsbury-allocated 'Counties' worked into Bristol on a regular basis with services to and from the North West. Here, on 1 August 1953, *County of Wilts* stands in the yard at Bristol Bath Road in preparation for its next turn of duty. *Norman Preedy Archive*

Above:
A 'County' at its best. A very clean *County of Wilts* climbs the 1-in-80 Nantyderry Bank with the 9.10am service from Liverpool to Plymouth on 7 March 1958, this being the outward leg of a 'double home' working to Newton Abbot. At this time No 1003 was allocated to Shrewsbury, which always provided one of its best engines for this turn. *R. O. Tuck / Great Western Trust collection*

Below
Now in rather less pristine condition, *County of Wilts* breasts the summit at Whiteball with the Saturdays-only 10.5am service from Kingswear to Wolverhampton on 18 August 1962. Although apparently still in good working order, it was withdrawn from Shrewsbury just two months later, on 22 October. *M. J. Fox*

1004 *County of Somerset*

Built	Swindon, October 1945
Named	August 1946
Double chimney fitted	April 1957
Allocations	Plymouth Laira from new
	Penzance, May 1950
	Shrewsbury, November 1951
	Wolverhampton Stafford Road, February 1953
	Swindon, February 1954
Withdrawn	21 September 1962 (first member of the class to be withdrawn)
Final mileage	657,523
Cut up	J. Cashmore, Newport, May 1964

Above:
No 1004 was completed at Swindon on 15 October 1945 and was named *County of Somerset* on 14 August 1946. Although mostly used on passenger services the class could often be seen on freights. Here the fifth 'County' built descends Tomperrow Bank, between Chacewater and Truro, with an up Class D express mixed freight on 8 May 1947. *B. A. Butt*

Above:
This is a fine study of No 1004 as it accelerates along the Great Western main line west of Chippenham with the 5.42pm semi-fast service from Chippenham to Bristol Temple Meads on 12 May 1953. This service was regularly used as an ex-Swindon Works running-in turn. *P. M. Alexander*

Below:
A regular Wolverhampton Stafford Road (84A) turn was the 'Cornishman', the 10.35am service from Penzance to Wolverhampton, seen here climbing Fishponds Bank, Bristol, on 6 August 1953 hauled by *County of Somerset*. The heavy train is being banked by Midland '4F' 0-6-0 No 44169. *P. Q. Treloar collection*

Left:
On a rather dull summer's evening on 13 July 1953, *County of Somerset* is in charge of the 6.35pm stopping service from Oxford to Banbury past Wolvercote Siding, just north of Oxford. The 'County' is probably working its way back to its home shed at Wolverhampton. The stock is in the then new BR standard suburban red livery. *E. D. Bruton / Great Western Trust collection*

Below left:
In February 1954, *County of Somerset* moved to Swindon (82C). Here it approaches Pengam Junction, Cardiff, on 2 June 1957 with the Sundays-only Sheffield to Swansea service. This was a regular Swindon turn for either a 'Castle' or a 'County', which took over at Swindon from an Eastern Region locomotive (usually a 'B1' 4-6-0) which had brought the train down from the North. *R. O. Tuck*

Above:
No 1004's right-hand nameplate. *R. H. G. Simpson*

Below
County of Somerset speeds past Iver, Bucks, with a fast service from Paddington to Bristol and Weston-super-Mare on 6 July 1957. Fitted with a double chimney in May 1957, it was the first 'County' to be withdrawn, on 21 September 1962. *E. R. Wethersett / Great Western Trust collection*

1005 *County of Devon*

Built	Swindon, November 1945
Named	July 1946
Double chimney fitted	December 1958
Allocations	Bristol Bath Road from new
	Bristol St Philip's Marsh, September 1960
Withdrawn	24 June 1963
Final mileage	710,034
Cut up	J. Cashmore, Newport, August 1964

Below:
No 1005 was completed on 6 November 1945 and was named *County of Devon* on 24 July 1946. Allocated from new to Bristol Bath Road, it rushes past Ealing signalbox in April 1946 with a service from Paddington to Bristol. *C. G. Stuart / Great Western Trust collection*

Above:
Not much cleaning being done here, as a rather grubby-looking *County of Devon* awaits its next turn of duty at Bristol Bath Road in September 1954. Six members of the class were allocated here at this time. *Great Western Trust collection*

Right:
No 1005, in BR mixed traffic lined-black livery, stands at Bristol Temple Meads *c*1954, having arrived with an up service from the South West. *P. Q. Treloar collection*

Above:
Having been repainted in BR lined-green livery at Swindon in October 1956, a very clean *County of Devon* receives attention at Bristol Bath Road on 7 February 1957. This was a Bristol-based locomotive for the whole of its working life, being allocated to Bath Road in November 1945; when that depot closed to steam on 12 September 1960 for conversion into a diesel depot No 1005 moved to Bristol St Philip's Marsh. *Ivo Peters*

Above right:
The 'Counties' worked services to and from most corners of the old Great Western system. Here *County of Devon* approaches Marazion station with an up empty stock train on 11 May 1959. It was fitted with a double chimney at Swindon in April 1957. In the background is Penzance (83G) locomotive depot. *Michael Mensing*

Right:
Another fine view of *County of Devon*, with nine on, as it powers its way up to Church Stretton with a Manchester–Plymouth service on 30 March 1963. Although devoid of a shedplate it was still working from Bristol St Philip's Marsh, from where it was withdrawn in June of the same year. *T. E. Williams*

1006 *County of Cornwall*

Built	Swindon, November 1945
Named	April 1948
Double chimney fitted	December 1958
Allocations	Plymouth Laira from new
	Carmarthen, June 1954
	Penzance, October 1954
	St Blazey, June 1960
	Plymouth Laira, October 1960
	Swindon, January 1963
Withdrawn	17 September 1963
Final mileage	687,685
Cut up	Coopers Metals, Sharpness, June 1964

Above:
No 1006 *County of Cornwall* stands at Newton Abbot with an up stopping service to Exeter in 1948. Completed on 15 November 1945, it was not named until 22 April 1948. In this picture the locomotive is still in Great Western lined-green livery, with its number painted on the front buffer-beam, but 'BRITISH RAILWAYS' has been applied to the tender. *Great Western Trust collection*

Below:
The 10.15am service from Penzance to Manchester arrives at Plymouth North Road on 16 May 1954, hauled by *County of Cornwall*. This was a regular turn for a Laira-based 'County'. *R. E. Vincent*

Above:
County of Cornwall was observed on station pilot duty at Plymouth North Road on 11 April 1956 and was in BR mixed traffic lined-black livery. Western Region allocation records show it had a brief spell away at Carmarthen between June and October 1954, but apart from this it was allocated in the South West for most of its working life. *F. M. Gates / Great Western Trust collection*

Below:
'Counties' saw regular use on local stopping services in the South West: here No 1006 heads the 3.40pm from Plymouth to Penzance, comprising three coaches and a parcels van. It climbs the grade up to Treverrin Tunnel near Lostwithiel on 13 June 1956. *Michael Mensing*

Above:
There is power in reserve as *County of Cornwall* and 'Castle' class 4-6-0 No 4091 *Dudley Castle* double-head the 8.20am service from Penzance to Paddington at Dainton Summit on 4 August 1958. The train is about to enter Dainton Tunnel.
T. E. Williams

Left:
An up service from Taunton to Paddington passes Sydney Gardens, Bath, on 13 August 1961, hauled by *County of Cornwall*. Fitted with a double chimney in December 1958, the locomotive was transferred in January 1963 to Swindon (82C), from where it was withdrawn in September.
Derek Cross

1007 *County of Brecknock*	
Built	Swindon, December 1945
Named	January 1948
Double chimney fitted	May 1957
Allocations	Bristol Bath Road from new
	Truro, January 1955
	Didcot, March 1961
Withdrawn	5 October 1962
Final mileage	658,967
Cut up	King & Sons, Norwich,
	November 1963

Above:

No 1007, as yet unnamed, powers the up 'Torbay Express' near Torquay in July 1946. Completed on 5 December 1945 and based from new at Bristol Bath Road, the locomotive was named *County of Brecknock* on 12 January 1948.
W. Potter / Great Western Trust collection

Below:

County of Brecknock waits to depart from Bristol Temple Meads in the early months of 1948 with an up service to Paddington. It is still in full Great Western lined-green livery with the GW crest on the tender. *Great Western Trust collection*

Above:
Now resplendent in BR lined-black livery, No 1007 departs from Salisbury on 8 March 1954, with a through service from Portsmouth to Bristol. At this time the locomotive was still allocated to Bristol Bath Road. *R. W. Beaton*

Below:
Fitted with a double chimney in May 1957, *County of Brecknock* departs light-engine from Penzance station on 24 July after arriving with a down service; it will run up to Penzance Long Rock (83G), where it will be serviced and turned in preparation for its next duty. From January 1955 until March 1961 this locomotive was allocated to Truro (83F). *Norman Preedy Archive*

Above:
On 16 May 1959, No 1007 was pictured climbing
to the summit of Tomperrow Bank between Truro and
Chacewater with the 4.15pm Truro-Penzance service.
Michael Mensing

Above:
The 'Counties' were also seen on parcels workings, as here:
No 1007 departs from Gwinear Road on 19 September
1959 with a down train. Shunting in the bay is ex-GWR
'4575' 2-6-2T No 4588. *P. Q. Treloar*

Above:
On a fine late-summer's evening, with hardly a cloud in the sky, *County of Brecknock* departs from St Erth in September 1959 with an up evening stopping service from Penzance to Plymouth. *P. Q. Treloar*

Right:
On 21 September 1959 No 1007 climbs away from Truro with a down goods. The introduction of diesels on West Country services saw it move to Didcot (81E) in March 1961, from where it was withdrawn in October 1962. *P. Q. Treloar*

1008 County of Cardigan

Built	Swindon, December 1945
Named	June 1947
Double chimney fitted	May 1958
Allocations	Old Oak Common from new
	Chester, October 1952
	Plymouth Laira, July 1958
	Penzance, December 1958
	Plymouth Laira, June 1961
	Neyland, September 1962
	Shrewsbury, February 1963
Withdrawn	3 October 1963
Final mileage	726,835
Cut up	Coopers Metals, Swindon, August 1964

Above:

No 1008 was completed at Swindon on 10 December 1945 and was named *County of Cardigan* on 13 June 1947. It was initially allocated to Old Oak Common, but moved to Chester in October 1952. It is seen here arriving at Oxford on 20 March 1953 with the 9.30am through service from Birkenhead to Bournemouth West. This was a regular turn at this time for a Chester (84K)-based 'County'. *Dr G. D. Parks*

Below:

A fine portrait of *County of Cardigan* taken at Cardiff Canton shed on 13 September 1953. The locomotive is receiving attention, hence the 'Not to be moved' sign on the front buffer-beam. It also seems to have become rather grubby in the six months since the previous photograph was taken. *Norman Preedy Archive*

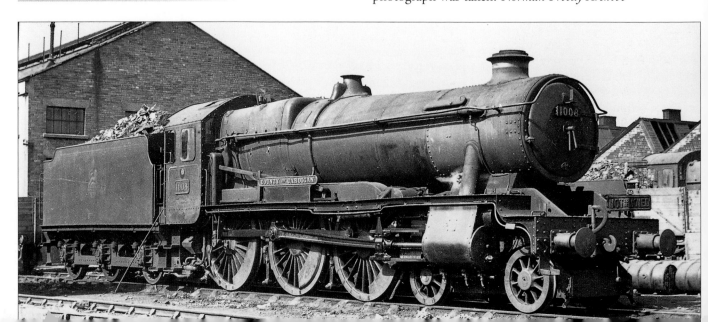

Right:
The 9.30am service from Bournemouth West to Birkenhead hauled by *County of Cardigan* is seen between Knowle & Dorridge and Widney Manor on 10 August 1957. The 'County' would have taken over from a Southern Region locomotive at Oxford. *Michael Mensing*

Right:
No 1008 was fitted with a double chimney in May 1958. Having been reallocated from Chester to Plymouth Laira in July 1958, the locomotive is shown leaving Chester with a through service to Paddington in June 1959. *E. N. Kneale*

Right:
County of Cardigan double-heading a service from Paddington to Plymouth with ex-Great Western 'Hall' 4-6-0 No 5941 *Campion Hall* at Parson's Tunnel, Dawlish, in the summer of 1960. After a period in the South West of England the 'County' moved in September 1962 to Neyland and then, in February 1963, to Shrewsbury, from where it was withdrawn on 3 October. *Great Western Trust collection*

Left:
No 1009 was completed at Swindon on 21 December 1945 and was named *County of Carmarthen* on 6 February 1948. It was originally based at Plymouth Laira but is seen here in early British Railways days, probably at Neyland shed, where it was allocated at that time. It is still in Great Western lined-green but has 'British Railways' painted on the tender. For a few months after Nationalisation it carried a painted 'W' suffix (indicating Western Region) under its brass cabside numberplates.
Great Western Trust collection

1009 *County of Carmarthen*

Built	Swindon, December 1945
Named	February 1948
Double chimney fitted	September 1956
Allocations	Plymouth Laira from new
	Neyland, October 1948
	Bristol Bath Road, January 1955
	Bristol St Philip's Marsh, September 1960
Withdrawn	1 February 1963
Final mileage	702,148
Cut up	J. Cashmore, Newport, August 1963

Below:
In 1954 *County of Carmarthen* underwent extensive testing to improve its draughting. It is seen here at Swindon on 21 November 1954, fitted with its experimental stovepipe double chimney and a wooden test shelter and coupled to Churchward dynamometer car No W7W. The tests saw the fitting of double chimneys and four-row superheaters to all members of the class.
P. Edwards / Norman Preedy Archive

Above:
Interestingly, despite being the test locomotive, No 1009 was actually the second 'County' to be fitted with the new-pattern elliptical double chimney in September 1956. (The first was No 1022, in May 1956.) It is seen in its new guise leaving Parson's Tunnel, near Teignmouth, with the 7.30am service from Paddington to Plymouth on 16 April 1957. *W. N. Lockett*

Below:
County of Carmarthen was allocated back to Bristol Bath Road in January 1955, where this low-level shot was recorded on 17 February 1957. It shows to good effect the fabricated-steel front boiler and smokebox mounting as fitted to the class. *Ivo Peters*

Above:
No 1009 leaves the then extensive layout at Newton Abbot with a service from Plymouth to Exeter, on 2 July 1957. The engine shed and locomotive works and carriage sidings are on the left of the picture, while the lines diverging away to the right are the Moretonhampstead and Teign Valley branch. *P. Q. Treloar collection*

Below:
Today Melksham is but a pale shadow of the typical Great Western country station seen here on 13 April 1960, as *County of Carmarthen* passes through with the diverted 10.10am service from Bristol to Weymouth. With the closure of Bristol Bath Road shed to steam in 1960 No 1009 moved to nearby Bristol St Philip's Marsh, from where it was withdrawn in February 1963. *P. A. Fry / Great Western Trust collection*

Right:
No 1010 *County of Carnarvon* passes Westbourne Park on 28 July 1948 with a fast service from Paddington to Plymouth. Completed at Swindon on 22 January 1946, it was named on 16 December 1947. The name was altered to *County of Caernarvon* on 16 November 1951.
C. G. Stuart / Great Western Trust collection

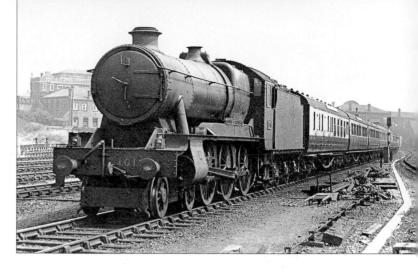

1010 *County of Caernarvon*

Built	Swindon, January 1946
Named	December 1947
	(as County of Carnarvon; County of Caernarvon from November 1951)
Double chimney fitted	January 1957
Allocations	Old Oak Common from new
	Plymouth Laira, December 1950
	Swindon, September 1959
	Neyland, September 1960
	Swindon, June 1961
Withdrawn	24 July 1964
Final mileage	779,055
Cut up	J. Cashmore, Newport, December 1964

Below:
Working flat out, *County of Caernarvon* (83G) climbs up the 1-in-60 bank at Frampton Crossing on 26 September 1953 with the 2.10pm, heavily loaded service from Cheltenham Spa to Paddington. It is in ex-works condition, having been released from Swindon just two days earlier after a heavy general repair. It had been reallocated from Old Oak Common to Plymouth Laira in December 1950. *G. Heiron*

Left:
In May 1955 *County of Caernarvon* visited Swindon Works again for another heavy general repair, this time it was repainted into BR lined-green livery. Looking absolutely superb, it stands in the works yard on 12 June 1955. It was the second 'County' to be turned out from Swindon in this livery, the first having been No 1017. *G. Wheeler*

Below left:
Comprising 12 coaches, the 11.50am service from Penzance to Paddington approaches Largin signalbox, between Bodmin Road and Doublebois, hauled by *County of Caernarvon* on 25 August 1956. *P. F. Bowles*

Above right:
Laira certainly looked after its locomotives. In superb condition *County of Caernarvon* climbs Dainton Bank with a service to Plymouth in the spring of 1959. It had been fitted with a double chimney during a heavy general repair in January 1957. *P. Q. Treloar collection*

Right:
No 1010 moved to Swindon (82C) in September 1959, and is seen there standing out of use alongside the stock shed on 7 February 1960. It was transferred to Neyland in September 1960 but returned to Swindon in June 1961. It was finally withdrawn in July 1964. *Ivo Peters*

Above:
An as yet unnamed No 1011 enters Sonning Cutting, east of Reading, with an up fast service from the South West *c*1946. This locomotive was completed at Swindon on 9 January 1946 and was named *County of Chester* on 13 November 1947. *Great Western Trust collection*

Below:
The unusual sight of a pair of 'Counties' double-heading an up service to Paddington, recorded at Exeter on 27 July 1948. No 1011 *County of Chester* leads No 1028 *County of Warwick*, both locomotives being still in Great Western livery and allocated to Bristol Bath Road. *W. Potter / P. Q. Treloar collection*

1011 *County of Chester*

Built	Swindon, January 1946
Named	November 1947
Double chimney fitted	November 1958
Allocations	Bristol Bath Road from new
	stored, February 1960
	Bristol St Philip's Marsh,
	September 1960
Withdrawn	21 November 1964 (last working
	member of the class)
Final mileage	728,610
Cut up	J. Cashmore, Newport, March 1965

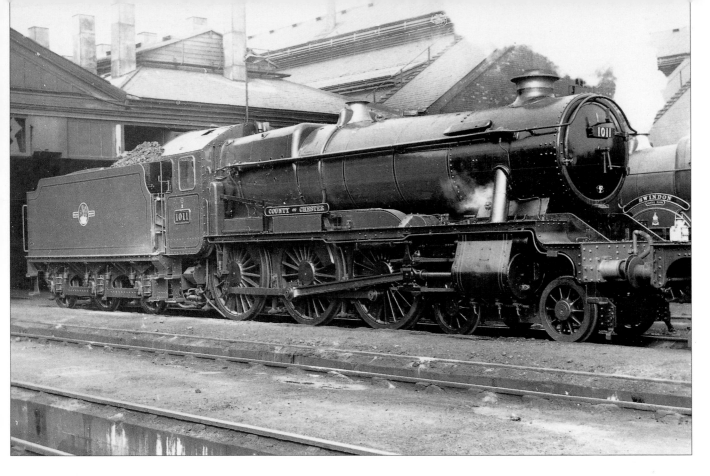

Above:
In pristine ex-works condition after a heavy intermediate repair, *County of Chester* (82A) stands in the shed yard at Swindon on 21 April 1957. *Norman Preedy*

Below:
A cracking high-level shot of *County of Chester* at speed between Pilning and Severn Tunnel on 9 May 1958, working the 11am service from Brighton and Portsmouth Harbour to Cardiff. It was fitted with a double chimney during a heavy general repair in November 1958. *Michael Mensing*

Left:
The 1.55pm service from Paddington to Swansea, hauled by *County of Chester*, passes under the former Barry Railway viaduct west of St Fagans on 19 June 1959. At this time it was unusual to see a 'County' working on a Paddington–South Wales service. *R. O. Tuck*

Below left:
No 1011 powers the 11.20am Plymouth–Taunton stopping service around the curves at Shaldon as it approaches Teignmouth on 2 August 1960. *Hugh Ballantyne*

Right:
No 1011's right-hand nameplate. *Great Western Trust collection*

Above:
A panoramic view of Penzance shed in 1959 featuring, from left to right, No 1011 *County of Chester*, 'Grange' 4-6-0 No 6855 *Saighton Grange* and No 1002 *County of Berks*. No 1011 was placed in store at Bath Road from February until September 1960 when it moved to St Philip's Marsh. Subsequently returned to traffic, it became the last working member of the class, finally being withdrawn from 82B in November 1964. *P. Q. Treloar*

1012 *County of Denbigh*

Built	Swindon, February 1946
Named	July 1946
Double chimney fitted	September 1957
Allocations	Old Oak Common from new
	Plymouth Laira, December 1950
	Swindon, September 1956
Withdrawn	24 April 1964
Final mileage	794,555 (highest recorded for the class)
Cut up	J. Cashmore, Newport, December 1964

Above:
No 1012 stands in the yard at Old Oak Common, its home shed, in May 1946. Turned out new from Swindon only on 8 February, the locomotive already looks rather dirty. It was named *County of Denbigh* on 3 July. *F. M. Gates / Great Western Trust collection*

Below:
The 7.15am service from Plymouth to Paddington, hauled by *County of Denbigh*, is seen passing Twyford *c*1948. *Maurice Earley*

Above:
A classic scene with *County of Denbigh* emerging from Parson's Tunnel on 10 June 1949 with the 5.30am service from Paddington to Penzance via Swindon, Bath and Bristol. Because of its early start from Paddington this service was known as the 'Newspaper' and, in spite of its express headlamp code, was not scheduled to reach Penzance until 4.25pm. *E. D. Bruton*

Right:
Superpower as *County of Denbigh* pilots 'King' class 4-6-0 No 6001 *King Edward VII* on the 3.30pm service from Paddington to Plymouth on 2 June 1951. The train is just passing the loco servicing point at Ranelagh Bridge on its way out of Paddington. *P. J. Lynch*

Above:
No 1012 waits at Taunton on 16 April 1956 with train 122, the 9.30am service from Paddington to Plymouth.
The locomotive carries an 83D (Plymouth Laira) shedplate, where it was allocated from December 1950 until transferred to Swindon in September 1956. It was fitted with a double chimney in September 1957. *P. M. Gates / Great Western Trust collection*

Below:
County of Denbigh is seen on Swindon MPD on 2 September 1962. By the time of is withdrawal from there on 24 April 1964 it had covered some 794,555 miles in service — the highest recorded mileage for any member of the class.
Great Western Trust collection

Above:

No 1013 was completed at Swindon on 11 February 1946 and allocated to Bristol Bath Road. Named *County of Dorset* on 14 January 1947, it is seen in Great Western lined-green livery passing Taplow with a down fast service from Paddington to Penzance. It moved from Bristol to the South West in December 1948, being allocated in turn to Plymouth Laira and Truro. *R. F. Dearden*

Below:

In November 1951 *County of Dorset* moved again, from the South West to Shrewsbury (84G), where it spent the next 11 years. It is pictured here at Bristol Temple Meads on 6 July 1955 in BR lined-black livery with the lion-and-wheel crest on the tender. *F. M. Gates / Great Western Trust collection*

1013 *County of Dorset*

Built	Swindon, February 1946
Named	January 1947
Double chimney fitted	February 1958
Allocations	Bristol Bath Road from new
	Plymouth Laira, December 1948
	Truro, May 1950
	Wolverhampton Stafford Road, October 1951
	Shrewsbury, November 1951
	Wolverhampton Stafford Road, October 1956
	Shrewsbury, December 1956
	Wolverhampton Stafford Road, December 1962
	Swindon, September 1963
Withdrawn	Swindon, 24 July 1964
Final mileage	630,737
Cut up	J. Cashmore, Newport, December 1964

Above:
No 1013's left-hand nameplate. *Great Western Trust collection*

Above right:
No 1013 enters Platform 2 at Chester General on 31 July 1963 with the early-morning parcels service from Shrewsbury. At this time allocated to Wolverhampton Stafford Road (84A), it moved to Swindon in September 1963. *S. D. Wainwright*

Below:
County of Dorset received its double chimney during a heavy general overhaul at Swindon in February 1958. It passes through Leamington Spa on 29 September 1962 with an up Class C mixed freight working. *Great Western Trust collection*

Below right:
A different view of Chester General, recorded on 10 August 1963 as *County of Dorset* departs with the 4.30pm service to Paddington from Birkenhead. This high viewpoint shows to good effect the clean lines of the Hawksworth straight-sided tender. No 1013 was finally withdrawn from Swindon (82C) in July 1964. *S. D. Wainwright*

1014 *County of Glamorgan*

Built	Swindon, February 1946
Named	March 1948
Double chimney fitted	November 1956
Allocations	Bristol Bath Road from new
	Bristol St Philip's Marsh, September 1960
	Neyland, September 1961
	Shrewsbury, April 1963
Withdrawn	24 April 1964
Final mileage	756,762
Cut up	J. Cashmore, Newport, December 1964

Below:
No 1014 *County of Glamorgan*, completed at Swindon on 18 February 1946,
passes Acton Yard with an up fast service from the South West on 8 May
1948. The locomotive, which was named on 15 March 1948, is still in
Great Western lined-green but has 'BRITISH RAILWAYS' painted on the tender.
C. G. Stuart / Great Western Trust collection

Right:
Allocated from new to
Bristol Bath Road, No 1014
departs from Saltford with an up
local service on the lovely summer's
evening of 8 June 1949. *R. C. Riley*

Below right:
County of Glamorgan makes a
dramatic departure from
Chippenham with the 5.5am
service from Paddington to
Plymouth via Bath and Bristol
in April 1950. Mail pick-up gear
and a GPO lineside hut can be seen
on the right. *P. M. Alexander*

Left:
The 8.20am service from Weston-super-Mare to Paddington, hauled by a very clean *County of Glamorgan*, stands at Bristol Temple Meads on 24 September 1951. The locomotive is in BR mixed-traffic lined-black livery, with red backing on the cabside number and nameplates, and carries an 82A (Bristol Bath Road) shedplate. *J. D. Mills*

Below left:
County of Glamorgan works hard as it passes Abergavenny Junction signalbox on the 1-in-82 climb up to Llanvihangel with the 10.5am service from Penzance to Liverpool on 8 September 1952. The 'Counties' were good performers on these cross-country services. *P. M. Alexander*

Above:
No 1014 was fitted with a double chimney during a heavy general repair in November 1956. Reallocated from Bristol St Philip's Marsh to Neyland in September 1961, the locomotive is seen at Carmarthen on 12 September 1962. It was withdrawn from Shrewsbury in April 1964. *Great Western Trust collection*

Above:
County of Glamorgan heads a Plymouth–Manchester service at Stapleton Road, Bristol, in May 1959. The Great Western Society is currently building a replica of this locomotive in its later, double-chimney form. *Great Western Trust collection*

1015 *County of Gloucester*

Built	Swindon, March 1946
Named	April 1947
Double chimney fitted	November 1958
Allocations	Old Oak Common from new
	Plymouth Laira, December 1950
	Swindon, September 1959
	Didcot, August 1961
	Plymouth Laira, October 1962
Withdrawn	13 November 1962
Final mileage	724,192
Cut up	J. Cashmore, Newport, May 1964

Above:
No 1015 *County of Gloucester* stands alongside the water tower at Truro on 24 June 1951. Completed on 1 March 1946, it was named on 16 April 1947. Allocated from new to Old Oak Common, it moved to Plymouth Laira in December 1950. *B. Eccleston / P. Q. Treloar collection*

Below:
In very clean BR mixed-traffic black livery and complete with smokebox numberplate and 83D (Plymouth Laira) shedplate, *County of Gloucester* departs from Penzance on 15 June 1951 with the up 'Cornish Riviera', the 9.45am service to Paddington. *P. J. Kelley*

Above:
The Plymouth-based 'Counties' worked a variety of trains including main-line, intermediate, freight and parcels services. Here, *County of Gloucester* departs from Dawlish *c*1953 with the up 'Torbay Express', the 11.25am service from Kingswear to Paddington. *A. C. Roberts / Great Western Trust collection*

Below:
No 1015 approaches Plymouth on 5 August 1956 with the Sundays-only 1.20pm service from Penzance to Paddington. *T. E. Williams / Great Western Trust collection*

Above:
County of Gloucester was fitted with a double chimney in November 1958 and is seen so equipped at Old Oak Common on 15 March the following year. In September 1959 it moved from Plymouth Laira to Swindon.
Great Western Trust collection

Centre left:
No 1015's right-hand nameplate.
P. Q. Treloar collection

Left:
A down stopping service from Didcot to Swindon hauled by *County of Gloucester* approaches Wantage Road station in June 1962. This was to be the locomotive's last summer; on 15 October 1962 it moved from Didcot to Plymouth Laira, from where it was withdrawn on 13 November.
W. Turner

1016 *County of Hants*

Built	Swindon, March 1946
Named	September 1946
Double chimney fitted	March 1957
Allocations	Wolverhampton Stafford Road from new
	Shrewsbury, December 1951
	Wolverhampton Stafford Road, February 1952
	Shrewsbury, October 1952
Withdrawn	17 September 1963
Final mileage	642,078
Cut up	T. W. Ward, Sheffield, January 1964

Right:
No 1016 *County of Hants* departs from Wrexham on a cold and snowy 1 March 1947 with the mid-day service from Birkenhead to Paddington. Initially allocated to Wolverhampton Stafford Road, it had been completed at Swindon on 12 March 1946 and received its name in September of that year. *Geoffrey J. Jefferson / Great Western Trust collection*

Below:
A superb view of *County of Hants* in GWR days as it departs from Chester General with a through service from Birkenhead to Paddington. The locomotive seems to be in typical postwar grubby condition. *Eric Treacy*

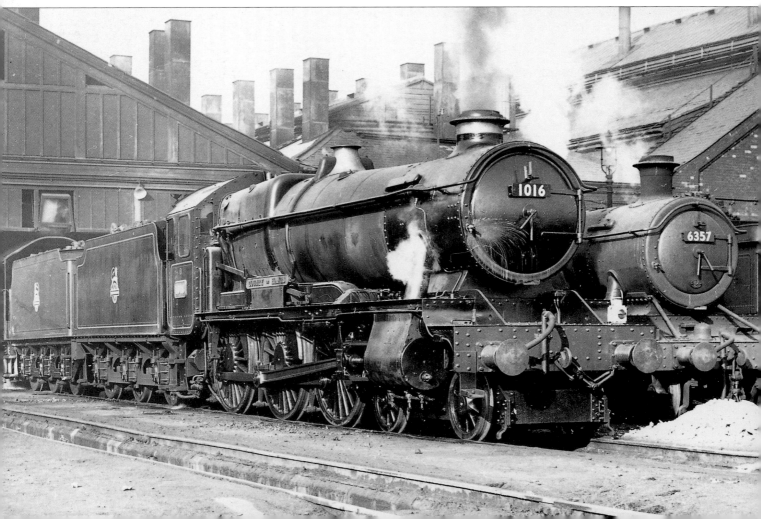

Left:
No 1016 passes Shipton for Burford on what is now known as the 'Cotswold Line', with a stopping service from Worcester to Oxford on 9 April 1950. The use of a 'County' on this route was a relatively rare occurrence. *P. A. Wells*

Below left:
In October 1952 *County of Hants* was allocated to Shrewsbury. Here it is seen, minus shedplate, outside the running shed at Swindon on 12 January 1953, having just visited the works for a heavy intermediate overhaul. Interestingly it retains red-backed name- and numberplates. *P. Edwards / Norman Preedy Archive*

Above right:
A very clean *County of Hants* makes a fine sight at Ruabon on 9 August 1956 with the 2.47pm departure, a stopping service from Shrewsbury to Chester. In 1956 there were five members of the class allocated to Shrewsbury. *Brian Morrison*

Right:
County of Hants waits in the middle road at Bath Spa on 7 March 1957 while on an ex-works running-in turn back to Swindon. It had just been fitted with its double chimney during a heavy general repair. *R. C. Riley*

Right:
Shrewsbury certainly kept its locomotives clean. Here, on 31 July 1957, a sparkling *County of Hants* speeds along the sea wall at Teignmouth with the 8am service from Plymouth to Crewe. *T. Lewis / Norman Preedy Archive*

1017 *County of Hereford*	
Built	Swindon, March 1946
Named	March 1946
Double chimney fitted	March 1959
Allocations	Wolverhampton Stafford Road from new
	Shrewsbury, November 1951
	Wolverhampton Stafford Road, May 1955
	Shrewsbury, January 1957
	Plymouth Laira, December 1960
	Shrewsbury, March 1961
Withdrawn	19 December 1962
Final mileage	601,066
Cut up	T. W. Ward, Sheffield, December 1963

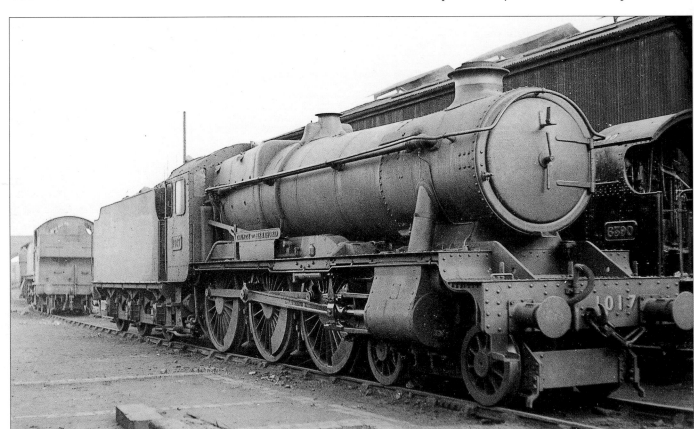

Above:
Passing the site of Rhosrobin Halt on its climb to Wrexham, *County of Hereford* powers the 2.35pm service from Birkenhead to Paddington on 18 April 1960. The train is formed of six BR Mk1 coaches in BR chocolate and cream livery.
Michael Mensing

Below:
County of Hereford moved once again to Shrewsbury in January 1957 and is seen here at Bristol Temple Meads later that year with the 2.55pm service from Paignton to Wolverhampton. It was repainted in BR lined-green livery in 1955.
J. P. Wilson / Great Western Trust collection

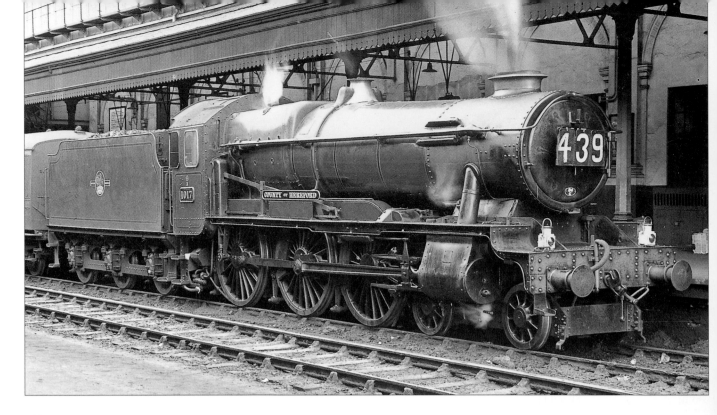

Above:
Having been fitted with a double chimney during a heavy general repair at Swindon in March 1959, No 1017 pauses at Exeter St Davids with a through train from Liverpool to Plymouth on 18 September. *C. F. H. Oldham / Great Western Trust collection*

Below:
A pair of 'Counties' captured on camera at Chester on 7 June 1962. In the foreground is *County of Hereford*, while beyond is No 1016 *County of Hants*; both were allocated to Shrewsbury (84G) at the time. This was to be the last summer in service for No 1017, which was withdrawn on 19 December. *J. R. Carter*

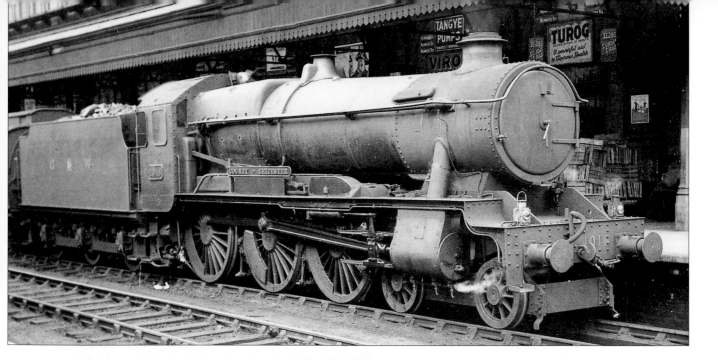

1018 County of Leicester

Built	Swindon, March 1946
Named	April 1946
Double chimney fitted	January 1958
Allocations	Newton Abbot from new
	Penzance, December 1950
	Shrewsbury, November 1951
	Wolverhampton Stafford Road, December 1952
	Plymouth Laira, September 1954
	Penzance, November 1954
	Plymouth Laira, June 1960
	Penzance, November 1960
	Wolverhampton Stafford Road, July 1961
	Didcot, October 1961
Withdrawn	27 September 1962
Final mileage	680,979
Cut up	King & Sons, Norwich, November 1963

Above:
Newton Abbot-allocated No 1018 *County of Leicester* stands at Reading General *c*1947 with a fast service for the South West. Completed on 23 March 1946, it was named on 2 April 1946. It is still in full Great Western lined-green livery but like many locomotives at this time has suffered from a shortage of cleaning staff.
Great Western Trust collection

Below:
In December 1950 *County of Leicester* was transferred from Newton Abbot to Penzance. Here, on 13 June 1951, it passes Gwinear Road with an up freight from Penzance Long Rock Yard.
P. J. Kelley

Above:
After moving from Penzance to Shrewsbury in 1951 and then to Wolverhampton in 1952, *County of Leicester* returned to the South West in September 1954, being reallocated first to Plymouth Laira and then, in November, to Penzance. Fitted with a double chimney in January 1958, it is seen here crossing Angarrack Viaduct, between Hayle and Gwinear Road, with the 1.55pm service from Penzance to Truro on 9 April 1960. *P. Q. Treloar*

Left:
In this photograph, taken on 30 July 1960, No 1018 is again hard at work, this time piloting 'Hall' 4-6-0 No 5997 *Sparkford Hall* up Dainton Bank with the 8.35am service from Liverpool to Plymouth. The train is nearing the top of the 1-in-38 climb to the tunnel. *Hugh Ballantyne*

Right:
A regular turn for a Penzance 'County' was the 4.20pm stopping service to Plymouth, on which working *County of Leicester* is seen arriving at Lostwithiel on 22 September 1959. In July 1961 the locomotive left the West Country for good, moving once again to Wolverhampton. *P. Q. Treloar*

Below:
No 1018 winds its way out of Shrewsbury on 23 June 1962 with the 11.40am from Birkenhead to Paddington. This was its last summer in action, as it was withdrawn from Didcot on 27 September.
John S. Whiteley

1019 *County of Merioneth*

Built	Swindon, April 1946
Named	from new
Double chimney fitted	March 1959
Allocations	Newton Abbot from new
	Penzance, August 1946
	Newton Abbot, October 1948
	Penzance, December 1950
	Shrewsbury, November 1951
	Wolverhampton Stafford Road, December 1952
	Swindon, February 1954
	Neyland, September 1960
	Swindon, February 1962
	Shrewsbury, September 1962
Withdrawn	11 February 1963
Final mileage	662,550
Cut up	J. Cashmore, Great Bridge, January 1964

Above:
The final 11 'Counties', Nos 1019-29, were named on completion. Fresh from Swindon Works, where it had been completed just a few days previously, No 1019 *County of Merioneth* prepares to depart from Swindon with an up stopping service to Didcot on 4 April 1946. This train was used for many years as an ex-works running-in turn. *H. C. Casserley / Great Western Trust collection*

Below:
A works-posed photograph of *County of Merioneth* taken at Swindon in February 1949. The locomotive is in full BR mixed-traffic lined black, being the first 'County' to be painted in this livery following Nationalisation, but has black backgrounds to its name- and numberplates. Note the NA (Newton Abbot) shed code stencilled on the front buffer-beam in Great Western style. *Ian Allan Library*

Above:

In December 1952 No 1019 moved to Wolverhampton Stafford Road (84A), being seen here hauling the 12.47am service from Hereford to Paddington passing under the 'Red Bridge' (Abingdon Road) at Hinksey, just south of Oxford, on 17 July 1953. The locomotive is in BR mixed-traffic lined black with red-backed name- and numberplates. *E. D. Bruton*

Below:

An atmospheric picture of a 'County' at speed as No 1019 passes through Little Somerford with an Easter extra from Paddington to South Wales *c*1955. *P. Q. Treloar collection*

Above:
An ex-GWR 'County' in former Great Central Railway territory. *County of Merioneth* runs through Leicester South with the 1.36pm service from Sheffield to Cardiff on 2 August 1958. It was not uncommon at this time for ex-Great Western 'Hall', 'Grange' and 'County' 4-6-0s to work cross-country services via Banbury and Woodford Halse through to Rugby and Leicester Central. *Colin Walker*

Below:
In February 1954 *County of Merioneth* was reallocated to Swindon (82C). Having been fitted with a double chimney while in the works for a heavy general repair in March 1959, it returned to traffic on the 27th and is here depicted at Reading on the following day, having arrived on an ex-works running-in turn. *R. Panting / Great Western Trust collection*

Above:
A few months later, on 12 July 1959, No 1019 and 'Castle' No 5027 *Farleigh Castle* double-head the 12.20pm Sundays-only service from Paddington to Weston-super-Mare, emerging from the short tunnel under Bathwick Terrace on the approach to Bath Spa. *Hugh Ballantyne*

Right:
In September 1960 No 1019 moved to Neyland for use on West Wales services but in February 1962 returned to Swindon, where it is seen in the shed yard on 27 May. It ended its days working from Shrewsbury, being withdrawn on 11 February 1963. *R. J. Henly*

1020 *County of Monmouth*

Built	Swindon, December 1946
Named	from new
Double chimney fitted	November 1958
Allocations	Chester from new
	Neyland, October 1948
	Shrewsbury, December 1948
	Neyland, February 1949
	Wolverhampton Stafford Road, June 1962
	Bristol St Philip's Marsh, September 1962
	Swindon, November 1963
Withdrawn	26 February 1964
Final mileage	599,291
Cut up	Hayes, Bridgend, June 1964

Above:

Completed on 14 December 1946, No 1020 *County of Monmouth* is seen on 10 September 1950 passing Pilning, on the descent into Severn Tunnel, with the 9.55am service from Paddington to Cardiff. The locomotive is in BR mixed-traffic lined black with red-backed name- and numberplates. *P. M. Alexander*

Below:

Having just spent 56 days in the works for a heavy casual repair, *County of Monmouth* stands in the yard at Swindon Works on 27 June 1954, awaiting a full repaint. This locomotive was allocated to Chester when new but moved to Neyland in October 1948. *Great Western Trust collection*

Right:
Neyland (87H)-allocated *County of Monmouth* comes off an up fish train at Cardiff Canton on the evening of 25 July 1955. This was a typical Neyland turn that changed locomotives here. Behind Canton Sidings signalbox is the huge Cardiff Canton locomotive shed. *R. O. Tuck*

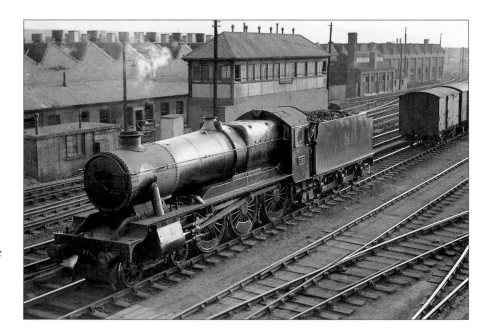

Below:
Fitted with a double chimney in November 1958, No 1020 is seen here near Haverfordwest on 5 August 1961 with the 6.50pm service from Neyland to Paddington.
Ian Allan Library

Right:
A detailed study of *County of Monmouth* standing in the yard at Tyseley in 1961. The 'X' on the cab denotes that this locomotive is capable of taking a heavier load than normally permitted. At this time still allocated to Neyland, it moved in June 1962 to Wolverhampton Stafford Road but ended its career at Swindon, on 26 February 1964.
Norman Preedy

1021 *County of Montgomery*

Built	Swindon, December 1946
Named	from new
Double chimney fitted	October 1959
Allocations	Old Oak Common from new
	Plymouth Laira, December 1950
	Penzance, March 1955
	Plymouth Laira, July 1955
	Swindon, October 1959
	Bristol St Philip's Marsh,
	November 1960
Withdrawn	1 November 1963
Final mileage	747,716
Cut up	Hayes, Bridgend, June 1964

Above:
Completed at Swindon on 19 December 1946, No 1021 *County of Montgomery* was allocated from new to Old Oak Common but in December 1950 moved to the South West, operating from Plymouth Laira. This fine view shows the locomotive departing Bristol Temple Meads with the 4.5pm service to Exeter in July 1951. *Ian Allan Library*

Below:
County of Montgomery approaches Bath Spa on the evening of 7 July 1954 with the 4.15pm service from Paddington to Plymouth via Bath and Bristol, comprising 11 coaches. *W. N. Lockett*

Right:
A final check by the crew of *County of Montgomery* as it stands in the yard at Penzance (83G) in April 1955. It had moved from Plymouth Laira to Penzance during the previous month. *Great Western Trust collection*

Above:
The 11am service from Penzance to Paddington hauled by *County of Montgomery* backs onto the 1.50pm through coaches from Kingswear at Exeter St Davids on Saturday 31 March 1956. The train also comprised through coaches from Plymouth Millbay. *P. Q. Treloar collection*

Above:
County of Montgomery pilots 'Warship' diesel-hydraulic No D806 *Cambrian* through Aller Junction on 4 September 1958 with a Nottingham–Plymouth working. Whether or not the diesel had failed is not recorded. *Derek Cross*

Left:
No 1021 hauls the 9.50pm overnight sleeper train from Paddington to Penzance between Gwinear Road and Hayle on 26 July 1958. *P. Q. Treloar*

Above:
County of Montgomery departs from St Erth *c*1958 with a service from Paddington to Penzance, the train comprising a mix of chocolate-and-cream and maroon BR Mk1 coaches. *P. Q. Treloar*

Below:
County of Montgomery was the last of the 'Counties' to be fitted with a double chimney, during a heavy general repair in October 1959, being seen ex works outside Swindon shed (82C) on 1 November. A year later it moved to Bristol St Philip's Marsh, from where it was withdrawn in November 1963. *R. H. G. Simpson.*

1022 *County of Northampton*

Built	Swindon, December 1946
Named	from new
Double chimney fitted	May 1956
Allocations	Penzance from new
	Plymouth Laira, October 1948
	Penzance, December 1950
	Chester, December 1951
	Shrewsbury, June 1958
Withdrawn	5 October 1962
Final mileage	590,659
Cut up	T. W. Ward, Sheffield, January 1964

Right:
County of Northampton moved from Penzance to Chester (84K) in December 1951. Heading the 3.10pm service from Paddington to Wolverhampton, it picks up water from Ruislip troughs on the former Great Western Birmingham cut-off route on 13 September 1952. *Norman Preedy Archive*

Below:
No 1022 *County of Northampton* was completed at Swindon on 24 December 1946. It is seen here in full Great Western livery climbing Tomperrow Bank, between Truro and Chacewater, on 17 April 1947 with a through service from Wolverhampton to Penzance, its home at the time. *B. A. Butt*

Below right:
No 1022 entered Swindon Works for a heavy general repair on 27 March 1956 and at the same time received an elliptical double chimney — the first 'County' to be so equipped. Here it poses in the yard at Swindon on 6 May in newly applied BR lined-green livery, while retaining the lion-and-wheel emblem on the tender. *Great Western Trust collection*

Above:
Having taken over from a Southern Region locomotive at Oxford, *County of Northampton* approaches the top of Hatton Bank with a through service from Bournemouth West to Birkenhead on 13 October 1956. *R. H. Short*

Below:
Again well into the climb of Hatton Bank, *County of Northampton* heads a cross-country service from Bournemouth West to Birkenhead on 12 January 1957. This fine broadside view shows to good effect the locomotive's double chimney. *T. E. Williams*

Right:
No 1022 moved from Chester to Wolverhampton Stafford Road in March 1957. Here it coasts down from West Bromwich to Swan Village with the 9.30am service from Bournemouth West to Birkenhead on 3 August 1957. *Michael Mensing*

Below:
In June 1958 *County of Northampton* was reallocated to Shrewsbury, being seen passing Saltney Junction, Chester, on 9 May 1959 with the 7.45am service from Paddington to Birkenhead. This locomotive was withdrawn from traffic in October 1962. *A. Wainwright / Great Western Trust collection*

Above:

Completed at Swindon on 1 January 1947, No 1023 *County of Oxford* spent most of its working life in the South West, being allocated at various times to Truro, Exeter, Plymouth and Penzance. Here, on 10 June 1949, it heads for Parson's Tunnel (the first of five tunnels between Teignmouth and Dawlish) with the 10.5am stopping service from Torquay to Exeter. *E. D. Bruton*

Below:

County of Oxford departs St Erth with the 4.15pm stopping train from Plymouth to Penzance on 15 September 1951. This service carried many schoolchildren *en route* and was known locally as the 'school train'. The locomotive is in BR mixed-traffic black livery with red-backed name- and numberplates and carries an 83F (Truro) shedplate. *B. A. Butt*

1023 *County of Oxford*	
Built	Swindon, January 1947
Named	from new
Double chimney fitted	May 1957
Allocations	Truro from new
	Exeter, November 1948
	Plymouth Laira, May 1950
	Penzance, December 1950
	Truro, August 1951
	Exeter, September 1959
	Swindon, March 1961
	Shrewsbury, September 1962
Withdrawn	1 March 1963
Final mileage	592,957
Cut up	Swindon Works, August 1963

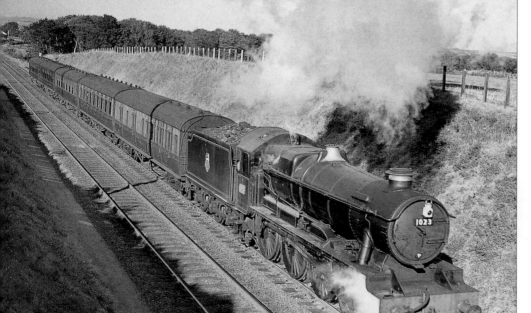

Above right:

During the summer months Penzance was a busy station, as is apparent from this photograph taken in July 1953. In the foreground *County of Oxford* prepares to depart with a London service calling at Truro and Plymouth, where extra coaches will be attached. *P. L. Melville*

Right:

This fine study shows *County of Oxford* crossing the viaduct at Liskeard on 10 July 1955 with the 10.40am service from Paddington to Penzance. *R. C. Riley*

Above:
No 1023 was fitted with a double chimney during a heavy general repair in May 1957. Here it arrives at Chacewater station on 20 May 1959 with the 4.15pm stopping service from Truro to Penzance, the eight-coach train comprising five passenger vehicles and three parcels vans. *Michael Mensing*

Below:
No 1023's right-hand nameplate. *D. H. Cape / P. Q. Treloar collection*

Above right:
The locomotive depot at Truro was opened by the Great Western Railway in 1900 and was closed to steam in March 1962, after which it was used as a diesel depot until complete closure in November 1965. A Truro-based locomotive from August 1951 until September 1959. *County of Oxford* awaits its next turn of duty in the shed yard on 18 September 1957. *P. Q. Treloar*

Right:
County of Oxford leaves Truro later the same day with the 4.15pm stopping service to Penzance. The locomotive moved from the South West to Swindon in March 1961 and thence in September 1962 to Shrewsbury, from where it was withdrawn on 1 March 1963. It was one of only two of the class to be cut up at Swindon Works, the other being No 1024. *P. Q. Treloar*

COUNTY OF OXFORD

1024 *County of Pembroke*

Built	Swindon, January 1947
Named	from new
Double chimney fitted	July 1958
Allocations	Wolverhampton Stafford Road from new
	Shrewsbury, October 1950
	Plymouth Laira, January 1951
	Old Oak Common, September 1952
	Chester, October 1952
	Bristol Bath Road, July 1958
	Bristol St Philip's Marsh, September 1960
	Swindon, November 1963
Withdrawn	8 April 1964
Final mileage	643,975
Cut up	Swindon Works, July 1964

Above:

No 1024 *County of Pembroke* was completed at Swindon on 9 January 1947. It is seen here at Chippenham on 22 July 1950 with an ex-works running-in turn, having been put into traffic the previous day after a heavy general repair. The livery is lined-black with red backing to the name- and numberplates. *Great Western Trust collection*

Below:

A broadside view of Chester (84K)-allocated *County of Pembroke* as it climbs Hatton Bank with a cross-country service to Wolverhampton *c*1956. The locomotive is still in BR lined-black livery, but the name- and numberplates have lost their red backgrounds. The locomotive had been transferred from Old Oak Common in October 1952. *P. Q. Treloar collection*

Above:
In July 1958 No 1024 was fitted with a double chimney, as seen at Didcot at the head of the 10.20am stopping service from Swindon on the 12th of that month. This duty was used by Swindon as an ex-works running-in turn. *C. G. Stuart / Great Western Trust collection*

Below:
In July 1958 *County of Pembroke* was reallocated to Bristol Bath Road, beings seen passing West Ealing *en route* to Paddington on 26 August with the 11.45am service from Bristol. *C. G. Stuart / Great Western Trust collection*

Left:
Still carrying an 82A (Bristol Bath Road) shedplate, *County of Pembroke* waits at Cardiff General on 4 March 1961. The closure of Bath Road shed to steam in September 1960 saw many of its remaining locomotives transferred to nearby St Philip's Marsh (82B). *Great Western Trust collection*

Below:
No 1024 rests at St Philip's Marsh on 11 August 1963. Although somewhat grubby and devoid of a shedplate, it appears still to be in good running order. It moved to Swindon (82C) in November 1963 and was withdrawn on 8 April 1964, being cut up at the works during July. *D. J. Wall*

1025 *County of Radnor*

Built	Swindon, January 1947
Named	from new
Double chimney fitted	August 1959
Allocations	Wolverhampton Stafford Road from new
	Shrewsbury, November 1950
Withdrawn	18 February 1963
Final mileage	601,069
Cut up	J. Cashmore, Great Bridge, January 1964

Above:
No 1025 *County of Radnor* was completed on 20 January 1947. When new it was allocated to Wolverhampton Stafford Road, moving in November 1950 to Shrewsbury, where it was to spend the rest of its working life. In this view, recorded at Oxford on 8 May 1954, the locomotive is in BR lined black but without the short-lived red-backed name- and numberplates. *Great Western Trust collection*

Below:
A light load for a 'County' as No 1025 leaves Chester with the 5.50pm stopping service to Ruabon on 8 September 1954. On the left is the Chester No 6 signalbox.
P. Q. Treloar collection

Left:
Seen near Solihull, *County of Radnor* heads the 9.30am restaurant-car service from Bournemouth West to Birkenhead on Saturday 10 August 1957. The Western Region locomotive would have taken over from a Southern Region locomotive at Oxford. *Michael Mensing*

Left:
No 1025 approaches Leamington Spa on 8 May 1958 with a down parcels service from London. It is in BR lined-green livery and has the later-type BR crest on the tender. *Michael Mensing*

Below left:
The 3.18pm Paddington–Wolverhampton semi-fast service nears the summit of Hatton Bank behind *County of Radnor* on Saturday 14 June 1958. The locomotive was fitted with a double chimney in August the following year. *Michael Mensing*

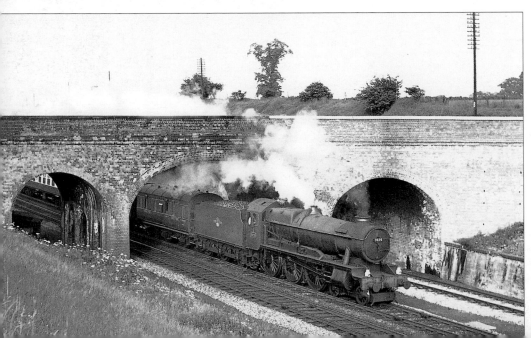

Above right:
On 2 July 1960 No 1025 passes Hinksey Yard, south of Oxford, with a Summer Saturdays-only service from Weymouth to Wolverhampton. *J. F. Loader / Great Western Trust collection*

Right:
Hauling quite a load, *County of Radnor* is well away from its home shed of Shrewsbury as it passes milepost 209½ at Teignmouth on 7 August 1960 with the 10.20am Sunday service from Plymouth to Paddington. The locomotive was withdrawn from traffic on 18 February 1963. *Hugh Ballantyne*

1026 *County of Salop*

Built	Swindon, January 1947
Named	from new
Double chimney fitted	October 1958
Allocations	Old Oak Common from new
	Plymouth Laira, September 1952
	Bristol Bath Road, February 1953
	Chester, February 1954
	Shrewsbury, October 1955
Withdrawn	13 September 1962
Final mileage	621,007
Cut up	T. W. Ward, Sheffield, January 1964

Above:
Completed at Swindon on 31 January 1947, No 1026 *County of Salop* is pictured on 17 July 1951 at its then home shed of Old Oak Common. The livery is difficult to discern beneath the grime but is probably BR mixed-traffic black. *F. M. Gates / Great Western Trust collection*

Below:
County of Salop pauses at Oxford in 1951 with an up stopping service, probably to London. The locomotive moved from Old Oak Common to Plymouth Laira during September 1952. *R. H. G. Simpson*

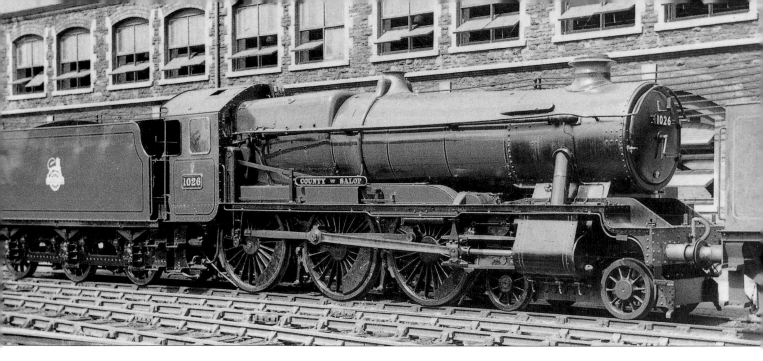

Above:
No 1026 entered Swindon Works in August 1956 for a heavy intermediate repair, from which it emerged in BR lined green, as seen on 18 September 1956. At this time the locomotive was allocated to Shrewsbury (84G). It returned to Swindon for a heavy classified repair in October 1958, when it was fitted with a double chimney. *G. Wheeler*

Right
County of Salop passes Hawthorns Halt at Handsworth Junction, Birmingham, on 25 March 1961 with the 9.30am through service from Bournemouth West to Birkenhead. This was a regular turn for a Shrewsbury 'County', as depicted in a number of earlier views. *Michael Mensing*

Right:
Busy times at Chester General as No 1026 departs with a Birkenhead–Paddington service on 20 May 1961. The locomotive was withdrawn from service at Shrewsbury on 13 September 1962. *A. Bryant*

Left:
No 1027 *County of Stafford* was completed at Swindon on 11 March 1947 and was allocated to Westbury. Here, on Saturday, 6 September 1947, the locomotive traverses the Thames Valley near Ruscombe with the 6.30am up fast service from Weymouth to Paddington. During its time at Westbury it was used almost exclusively on trains connecting these two destinations. *Great Western Trust collection*

1027 *County of Stafford*

Built	Swindon, March 1947
Named	from new
Double chimney fitted	August 1956
Allocations	Westbury from new
	Neyland, November 1950
	Bristol Bath Road, October 1959
	Bristol St Philip's Marsh, September 1960
	Neyland, April 1962
	Swindon, September 1963
Withdrawn	25 October 1963
Final mileage	650,666
Cut up	Coopers Metals, Sharpness, January 1964

Below:
No 1027 at Newbury, in charge of the 12.30pm return service from Paddington to Westbury, on a rather dull 5 January 1948. In the bay on the right is the station pilot, '2251' 0-6-0 No 3212, while on the left is ex-MSWJ 2-4-0 No 1334 on the Lambourn Valley service. *M. Yarwood / Great Western Trust collection*

Above right:
Still in full Great Western lined-green livery on 10 April 1948, *County of Stafford* waits at Reading with what is believed to be the 6.30am up fast service from Weymouth to London. *Great Western Trust collection*

Above:
In November 1950 *County of Stafford* was reallocated to Neyland (87H), where it stayed until 1959. Here, in May 1951, the locomotive trundles through Llantrisant with the 8.48am parcels and empty van service from Fishguard to Paddington. In BR lined-black livery, it has been fitted with a smokebox numberplate and shedcode plate.
P. Q. Treloar collection

Above:
A rather grubby *County of Stafford* at Carmarthen station on 25 June 1955. *F. M. Gates / Great Western Trust collection*

Below:
County of Stafford was the second member of the class to be fitted with the new-design double chimney, during a heavy general repair in August 1956. In October 1959 it moved from Neyland to Bristol Bath Road (82A), where it is seen in April 1960 awaiting its next turn of duty. It moved back to Neyland in April 1962 but finished its days at Swindon, from where it was withdrawn on 25 October 1963. *Great Western Trust collection*

1028 *County of Warwick*

Built	Swindon, March 1947
Named	from new
Double chimney fitted	August 1958
Allocations	Old Oak Common from new
	Bristol Bath Road, January 1948
	Bristol St Philip's Marsh,
	September 1960
	Swindon, November 1963
Withdrawn	2 December 1963
Final mileage	723,639
Cut up	Birds, Swansea, May 1964

Above:
No 1028 *County of Warwick* was completed at Swindon on 26 March 1947 and was initially allocated to Old Oak Common. It emerges from Twerton Tunnel near Bath on 28 May 1949, with the 4.15pm service from Paddington to Bristol. It has been fitted with a smokebox numberplate but does not as yet have a BR shedplate. *R. C. Riley*

Below:
In January 1948 No 1028 moved from Old Oak Common to Bristol Bath Road. It heads through Cholsey Cutting in the early 1950s with a fast service from Bristol to Paddington. *D. Hepburn-Scott*

Above:
A classic view of *County of Warwick* near Uphill Junction *c*1955 with the 11-coach 11.20am Sundays-only train from Penzance to Wolverhampton. W. N. Lockett

Right:
No 1028's left-hand nameplate. *Great Western Trust collection*

Below:
An undated photograph, taken *c*1956, of *County of Warwick* making its way to Ranelagh Bridge for servicing, having worked into London with the 11.45am service from Bristol to Paddington. In BR lined-green livery, it retains the earlier lion-and-wheel tender emblem. *Great Western Trust collection*

Above:
Fitted with a double chimney in August 1958, *County of Warwick* looks to be in excellent condition at Newbury Racecourse on 27 July 1963. This locomotive is being turned after arriving with a race special from Paddington. *D. Tuck / Great Western Trust collection*

Below:
Pictured towards the end of its working life, No 1028 climbs Hatton Bank with a down freight on 28 September 1963. By now allocated to Bristol St Philip's Marsh, it was withdrawn from traffic on 2 December. *Paul Riley*

Left:
No 1029 *County of Worcester* was the last 'County' to be built, being turned out by Swindon Works on 10 April 1947. When new it was allocated to Wolverhampton Stafford Road, where it was photographed in 1949. The 'X' below the route classification ('D') on the cabside denotes that this locomotive was permitted to take loads above those laid down in the working regulations. *Frank Moss*

1029 *County of Worcester*

Built	Swindon, April 1947
Named	from new
Double chimney fitted	May 1959
Allocations	Wolverhampton Stafford Road from new
	Neyland, December 1953
	Swindon, June 1961
Withdrawn	5 December 1962
Final mileage	555,216 (lowest recorded for class)
Cut up	J. Cashmore, Newport, November 1963

Above right:
Another early view of *County of Worcester*, emerging from the tunnel under the city wall at Chester with a service from Birkenhead to Paddington. It has been fitted with a smokebox numberplate but as yet does not have a shedplate. *Eric Treacy*

Below:
In BR mixed-traffic lined-black livery, No 1029 stands beneath the overall roof at Birmingham Snow Hill at the head of a semi-fast service on 30 June 1953. In December of that year it was reallocated to Neyland for use on West Wales services. *L. Hanson / Great Western Trust collection*

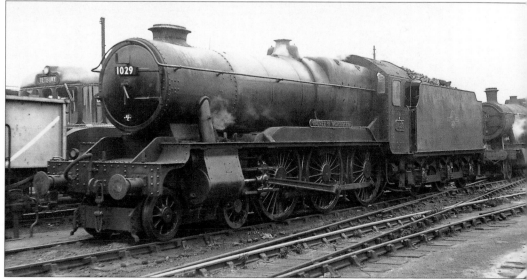

Right:
County of Worcester was fitted with a double chimney during a heavy casual repair in May 1959. In June 1961 it moved from Neyland to Swindon, where it is seen awaiting its next duty in the shed yard. It was finally withdrawn from traffic on 5 December 1962. *Great Western Trust collection*

Above:
No 1010 *County of Caernarvon* (82C) departs from Oxford on Saturday 20 July 1963 with the 11.5am service from Weymouth to Wolverhampton Low Level. This was one of the last four working members of the class, the others being Nos 1000, 1011 and 1013. Allocated to Swindon at this time, No 1010 was withdrawn from service on 24 July 1964.
G. T. Robinson

Left:
No 1013 *County of Dorset* was another of the last four to be withdrawn, on 24 July 1964. Having had a heavy casual repair at Wolverhampton Works in July 1963, it moved in September from Wolverhampton Stafford Road, where it had been allocated, to Swindon, where it is seen in the shed yard on 1 December. *Hugh Ballantyne*

Right:
Many of the 'Counties' were placed in store prior to being scrapped. Seen inside the roundhouse at Swindon on 26 July 1964 are Nos 1013 *County of Dorset* and 1000 *County of Middlesex*, both withdrawn earlier in the month; also here at this time was No 1010 *County of Caernarvon*. The locomotives illustrated have had their name- and numberplates removed prior to despatch to Cashmore's of Newport, where they would be cut up. *J. C. Heydon*

Below
Devoid of name- and numberplates, No 1019 *County of Merioneth* stands in the scrap line in the Gasworks sidings at Swindon on 24 March 1963, having been withdrawn from Shrewsbury on 11 February. It was cut up by Cashmore's, Great Bridge, in January 1964. *D. Tuck*

Above:

The 'County' swansong as *County of Chester* drops down from Sapperton Tunnel on its approach to Kemble with the SLS 'Last County' special from Birmingham to Swindon Works on 20 September 1964, its number once again carried on the buffer-beam. No 1011 was the last working member of the class, being officially withdrawn after the run; it was, however, reported subsequently on a number of workings, mainly freight trains in the Bristol/Swindon area. It was finally placed in store in November 1964 before being sold to Cashmore's at Newport but was not cut up until March 1965 — in retrospect an opportunity missed, but in the mid-1960s railway preservation was still in its infancy. *Hugh Ballantyne*